ZAZ

alurista

FLOWERSONG
PRESS

FlowerSong Press
McAllen, Texas 78501
Copyright © 2020 by Alberto Baltazar Urista Heredi

ISBN 978-1-953447-91-3
Library of Congress Control Number: 2020946864

Published by FlowerSong Press
in the United States of America.
www.flowersongpress.com

Set in Adobe Garamond Pro

Cover art by Mario Godinez
Typeset and design by Matthew Revert
www.matthewrevert.com

Dedication:

To all my relatives

Word Master
Word Maestro

Always in the Present Tense
You give us pause to inhale exhale
wisdom
beauty
sensuality
conscience

you b the one named tamed
Desolate Nazizona

Your heartbreaking questions
Teach us meaning

You make us One with All
Sacerdote of the Living Word

Heart. Soul. Blessing is u

—Denise Chávez is an Activist and Director of Libros Para El Viaje, an ongoing Refugee/Migrant/Asylum-seeker book initiative, and the author of The King and Queen of Comezón

"alurista es el mero mero, a 'root' Xicanx poet, the etymology of our post-colonial mind literature starts with this vato. These word-breaths are more than letters on paper—they are prophecies, clarities, unclarities, rage on page, and humo de copal on a warm spring day."

—Luis J. Rodriguez, author of "Borrowed Bones" and "My Nature is Hunger."

9   a whisper
10   AZ SB 1070 reeking
11   en imperial beach
12   huitzilopoxtli
13   tranquility hovers
14   circumstances all
15   yuh dieter paint
16   did I tell u
17   seed, cultivate
18   with respect
19   my toesie other
20   not doing
21   wisdom defies
22   reality
23   if one can measure
24   vat b in a b.a.?
25   homo novis
26   morning beckons
27   con caring
28   clear i b
29   mine b z awe
30   i may b a fossil
31   don't fit?
32   putatively
33   memorations.com
34   new pope
35   súdote bonito
36   played in denver
37   corner derexo

a whisper
at the end of my thoughts
old pain
new birth
ancient ashes
spark new flame
Zapatismo en Amerindia
"everything for everyone
nothing for us"

AZ SB 1070 reeking
fascists fumes
cactus curtains
rise racism
reels down
adobe streets
desolate nazizona

en imperial beach
flor de durazno
opens its petalos
solar brisa
its scent caresses

huitzilopoxtli
been cracking
toes tonantzin
roses bloom
healing

tranquility hovers
above thoughts
flowing arroyos
trickle past

circumstances all
require diligence
control well
lest naught overflow

yuh dieter paint
dreams manifest
color hues bright

did I tell u
jesus saves
moisés invests
ketzalcoatl xinga

seed, cultivate
tonantzin nurtures
blooms, fructifica
we learn, live
rejoice, longevity b

with respect
with reverence
we b grape full
inebriated with
life, laboriously
being one with all

my toesie other
self incarnate
lubricating
con pinceles
xicanos la desnudez
xicana vereda hums
a nuestros pies

not doing
clearly
monumental
task b hurdle
on z path

wisdom defies
a menudo
consensus comfort

reality
consensual
description
b illusive

if one can measure
its movement
it b all there
real here & now

vat b in a b.a.?
n a ph...di?
accumulated
degreed knowledge
wisdom???

homo novis
carpe diemo sea
¡písale!
dale gas
pa'lante
zaz mij@!

morning beckons
nuevos lares presage
bright light stroll
awakens new direcciones
ya salió tonatiuh

con caring
council aconséjate
smile sandia slice
spit the seeds

clear i b
inking my güey
through past

mine b z awe
anti ti hermosura
naked I stand

i may b a fossil
n i have a bone
2 bury within u

don't fit?
cast off?
clear closet
redress
b new u

putatively
shared lair
rendered couple
betrothed

memorations.com
cuarenta años
despúes nada
ha cambiado
war thrives
con petro

new pope
alisó roots
reaching deep
ríos subterráneos
lázaro risen
emplumado
izando banderas
floricantadas

súdote bonito

tinta roja

d la media noxe

metáfora pinta

tu rostro lexuza

luna creciente

d la media noxe

púrpuramarillo

d la media noxe

tus sonrientes labios

d la media noxe

sandía rojiverde

d la media noxe

bonito t sudo

played in denver
green gulf ball
one swing
one hoyo
voló bien

corner derexo
black ball
call pocket
sink
we win!

mis yemas
recuerdan
los dedos
d tus pies y manos
asi también tu xoya
cabello frondoso
sueños son
rientesbesos

los ríos
no ladran fronteras
mujer cruzemos
x
nuestros vástagos

encuentros inesperados
construyen pirámides
imágenes conocientes
ars vitae amoris

como la ola
va y viene
rebozante
tabléala
hasta la playa!
goza tus palmas
en la sombrita
coloréate!

ardilla madre
busca y encuentra
bellota ke alimente
ardillitas trankilas
lares ni ladran
los canes

ombligos n waists
abrazos cadereando
profunda lengua
sabroseándonos
d muslo a muslo
acupresionando
las plantas d
nuestros pies
licking calves
from ankle 2 knee
flower with me
dentro d tí
amo ergo sum

gallo cantaluz
amanecer seguro
feathers gathered
plumage present

realitińdiscript ion
mokeando la gota
flaca looking
work notŕound

tobillo sam
en cuncliyas
resa se us
a té walk

marbles
put down
within circle
tira tu balín

alza cue kiu
sale flexa
render target
travez
ojo claro

masamaié
tu güey, way
linea mariya
paĺante
derexo
yantas
ameríndias
caminemos

las malas it zat
nazizona
danzas
ecclesia stickas
de la pluma
vuelan rejas
caben, caven!
funda ciones

amer indian
whistle blow
cemanahua pueblo
xisme, rumor
has it zat
nazizona
alberganaciones
con plumas kkke
con rabos con
cascos policia
cos

maya mixteca
zapoteca tarasca
purepexa ya vas
uvas eva pisemos
bailemoslas
descalzos
garra´dan
las gua yabas
dulcemente

mound ver
none abre
tus ojos
clari fica
waxa,es
cuxa el
ferro, carril
ate, zorra
tu pill ow
a cuerda te

past

my prime

priming

my present

b now

here

naught

there

then

undocumented
mexicans slave
deported without
pay yo dues…
ke? taxes?

los cópteros de la migra
rugen lampareando
rojas, hambrientos
cruzamos el desierto

hasta los camellos
comen tuna
en lincoln acres
galopeando calles
pateando asfalto

ke vivan los muertos
ke mueran los ke se
creen muy vivos
a pus ké
la jodienda´taca
bajo ke no?
akí en tlaltipac
nomás! se alzan
los tuertos piratas

asuntos varios
bajo la mesa
best b dealt with
sin treacherous
patadas

el invierno tiburón
llega con tonatiuh
akí en San Juan Diego
estamos veraneando
no complaints
even though hawks
drool hovering
over doves

2 reasons ké opacan
nuestra jornada
brillan with heart
calurosamente

contigo soy una cania
con xanclas acoplados
con yanira l.a.

trabajo baja
hasta las plantas
descalzas
sin huaraxes

About the Author

Alberto Baltazar Urista Heredia, known as alurista, is a Chicano poet and activist. He was born in Mexico City and moved to San Diego with his family at the age of 13. He earned a BA in psychology and MA in literature from San Diego State University, and a PhD in literature from University of California, San Diego.

alurista is one of the first poets to blend English and Spanish languages in his writing, as well as various slangs of both. He is the author of many books, including *Xicano Duende: A Select Anthology* (2011), *Tunaluna* (2010), *Z Eros* (1995), and *Et Tu ... Raza?* (1995). He has written many essays and literary criticisms on the Chicano Movement and on Chicano culture, which have been widely published in anthologies, journals, and newspapers.

alurista is the co-founder of multiple academic and community organizations, such as Movimiento Estudiantil Chicano de Aztlán at San Diego State University, Concilio por la Justicia, Centro Cultural de la Raza, and the Department of Chicano Studies at San Diego State University. He has taught at California Polytechnic State University in San Luis Obispo, California, Escuela Tlatelolco in Denver, Colorado, and at the University of Texas at Austin. He has also lectured and read his poetry in venues throughout the world. His papers are held at University of Texas, Austin and at the California Ethnic and Multicultural Archives.